When Storms Come

To
Jim & Sherry
Here's to "Smooth Sailing"

When Storms Come

Finding Faith,
Hope, and Love
On Life's Restless Seas

By
John Buttrey II

Library of Congress Catalog Card Number: 98-93226

ISBN: 1-57502-943-X

LLMK PUBLISHING
1905 N. Sundown Lane
Anaheim, California 92807

Printed in the United States of America
By
Morris Publishing
3212 E. Hwy. 30
Kearny, NE 68847

It is with great respect and admiration
that this book is dedicated to

Homer Hailey

Who for so many years of Christian service,
has been an example of how to
faithfully endure life's many storms.
Though this book seeks to write about such,
he has lived and demonstrated
faith, hope, and love.
His many valuable contributions to
the cause of Christ
have been sources of
instruction and inspiration
which will serve many,
until our Lord's return.

Contents

Foreword

John Buttrey II, though a relatively young man, has learned three essentials of life: 1) Life is like a sea voyage; there will be calm days when all is tranquil and peaceful. Then there will be days of high winds and turbulent upheavals on life's sea. We need to expect both. 2) There is a divinely provided refuge for God's children in time of life's storms where one can find safety from destruction. 3) There is a time to learn the place of God's security and to prepare for taking advantage of this divine protection when the need arises.

The author used Paul's trip to Rome and the great storm that arose on that journey to illustrate and develop the essential truths of his thesis. He seeks to make the reader feel that he is traveling with Paul and his companion Luke on that exciting and perilous journey. He wants us to behold the flashes of lightning and hear the peals of thunder that follow. We sense the utter hopelessness of the situation as day after day there is no sight of sun, moon, or stars – we travel through those agonizing days of darkness wondering, *"When will all this cease?"*

In the midst of this seemingly hopeless situation, a word of hope is sounded. Paul stands forth encouraging the passengers and ship's crew with a word from God; in Him and the mighty working of His power not a soul will perish. But each must abide in His instruction; follow His orders. Paul demonstrates his faith in the promises of God by eating in their presence, and instructing the ship's crew to do the same. The ship was wrecked and destroyed, but out of the wreckage there was provided timbers on which those who could not swim might take hold and get to land. The journey ends. The travelers are on land. Delivered from the mighty storm. Saved by the grace of God and the provision of His providence, they can rest at ease and at peace.

From this experience of Paul's journey and the intrusion of the storm in the plans of the travelers, John draws his lessons. He likens life to Paul's journey to Rome. In the midst of life's journey storms strike, often with such severity that faith is severely tested, hope is shaken, and we begin to wonder if our love for God is sufficient to weather the storm. The author points to the promises of God as the place of true refuge. Faith in those promises which undergird the hope of triumph over all tests and trials is our guarantee of victory. The ship of life in which we travel may be shattered, but the pieces can be the means of saving us.

The writer urges everyone to make preparation early in life to meet and ride out the storms which will come, for they will come to us all at some time. Have you been able to meet successfully the storms of life? And are you meeting successfully those of the present? Does your ship of faith need undergirding to withstand the test? If so, I recommend that you read this book by John Buttrey II. You will not be disappointed.

Homer Hailey
Tucson, Arizona 1998

Acknowledgments

The book you are holding in your hands has evolved from a variety of different stages. The concept began as a forty-minute sermon, *"Surviving the Storms of Life."* From there it took the form of a little booklet. Eventually, it came to be what it is today. In the process, I discovered a new love... writing. Something I hope to improve on and continue in the future.

There are many people to thank who assisted greatly in getting this book put together. It would not have happened without their outstanding and much needed help.

I am very grateful and indebted to Homer Hailey for his insightful and honest review of the manuscript. Challenging me to improve what I had written and to rethink certain areas. I have done that, and it has helped a great deal in better communicating this message. Also for his inspiring me to continue preaching and writing. I am especially thankful for his provision of the wonderful foreword to this book.

Thank you to Van and Joyce Forsythe, and Don and Betty Lou Ware, for reviewing the manuscript and offering their helpful suggestions and words of encouragement. They each played a key role in making sure this project was done right, spending a lot of time reviewing several generations of the manuscript.

Many words of thanks to my sister-in-law Glenna Buttrey for her valuable assistance in editing and helping me properly say what I wanted communicated. To her husband, and my brother, Dan, thanks for watching the kids so she could work. And to my dad for his suggestions regarding this project.

Thank you to the good folks at Morris Publishing. Their helpful information and guidelines made the journey from sermon to book a real joy, and an actuality.

Special thanks must be given to my wife, Leigh, for her support of this project and my preaching. When she said, *"I do"* some fifteen years ago, preaching and writing were not a part of the package. Yet she remains supportive. I suppose that is what for better or worse is all about! And to my daughters Lindsay, Megan, and Kati, thank you for not complaining when Daddy would sometimes spend too much time at the computer typing.

A word of thanks must be given to my West Anaheim family. Their constant words of support and encouragement have been such an inspiration and help to me. They are truly a blessing from God and a source of joy in the journey. I hope in Christ, I can be the same for them.

Most importantly, thanks and praise be to God. He has done more for each of us than anyone could ever write about. His grace has been abundant in my life. He is the source behind all these words of thanks and the reason they are here given.

Oh give thanks to the Lord, for He is good,
For His lovingkindness is everlasting.
Psalm 107:1 (NASB)

Life's Storms

Setting sail through life
Fair weather will not always be
Skies can grow dark and clouds appear
And tempestuous grow the seas.

The ship will creak and moan
The masts and sails will strain
And days you thought the sun would shine
Will be nothing more than rain.

But hold on tight and keep your course
A promised rest awaits
It's worth your time and constant fight
Though a storm your life may take

With Faith and Hope as anchors
And a love that's firm and strong
You'll soon be landing at the place
The Faithful...
For eternity...
Belong.

John Buttrey II

Introduction

With eager and joyful anticipation of better times and better days one songwriter penned these familiar words...

> *O they tell me of a home far beyond the skies,*
> *O they tell me of a home far away.*
> *O they tell me of a home where no storm clouds rise,*
> *O they tell me of an unclouded day.*[1]

Sounds like a wonderful place, doesn't it? A home far away where no storm clouds rise! We sing about heaven. We read about heaven. Most of us can't wait for that home far away. The problem is... we're not there yet.

There is a journey through this life that must be sailed. A journey that is often filled with cloudy days. Many times those cloudy days turn dark and threatening. The rrrumbling sounds of thunder can begin to be heard echoing all around us, and we find ourselves in the midst of bad weather, looking for shelter and dealing once again with one of life's many storms.

We all experience the storms of life. Throughout the years of our life, they come and go. One minute the sun is shining, the air is fresh, the sky is clear; then in a very short time, almost without warning, the clouds start moving in... it starts getting dark and cold... and often before we have time to prepare for it, the storm is upon us, with all of its disruptive turbulence.

The storms of life bring with them many different things: loss, sickness, disappointment, sorrow, discouragement, loneliness, depression, pain... With the storms come questions, confusion, and doubts. Most commonly expressed by a single word question, *"Why?"*

"Why me?"
"Why my child?"
"Why would God allow this to happen?"

Whether we want to admit it or not, we all need to realize that life will always have difficult times. There will be times when life will not seem to make sense. And, there will be times of stormy weather, which to some may seem unfair. So what do we do? What do you do about the storm that may be raging in your life right now? And what about those that may come in the future?

Many would say preparing for the storms is important, and that is certainly true. Advanced preparation is a real key to faithful endurance. However, sometimes it seems like no matter how hard you prepare for a storm, you are never really quite ready for its destructive impact. Despite all the diligent preparation, storms still have a way of leaving their damage.

Perhaps more important than preparing for the storms is how we weather them. How we handle ourselves in the midst of their strong and destructive winds. Properly weathering life's storms is critical. The rough weather of life can affect our faith, our hope, and possibly our ability to love. At times, it even affects our ability to cope with life itself.

There is a way, I believe (though not always easy), to prepare ourselves; and at the same time find strength and endurance in weathering the difficult times. It is a way of handling life's many storms which seem to do their best to blow us off course. Call it a survival tip for handling the storms of life.

However, I should warn you, this survival tip will not take away the pain. It will not take away the disease. It will not stop the tears. It will not even answer all the questions. You're probably wondering, *"So what good is it?"* Good question. With all the things it will not do, it almost seems worthless. Yet,

xvi

it is what it will do that makes it so valuable. I believe this survival tip when practiced...

- Will keep our **faith** alive... and with faith comes vision and direction.
- Will give us **hope**... and with hope comes endurance.
- Will remind us of God's incredible **love**... and with love comes comfort.

Faith, Hope, and Love. These are three essential keys to help us survive any storm, no matter how mild or violent the storm may be. Call them anchors for maintaining stability during life's tempests. However, before I share this survival tip with you, we are going to have to work our way through, of all things, a storm!

Through the pages of this book, I want to take you on a perilous and turbulent journey through a very dangerous and life threatening storm. Our journey is found in the Bible; in the twenty-seventh chapter of the book of Acts. Through the words of that text, the author, Luke, takes us aboard a ship bound for Italy.

With incredible detail and description, Luke records nearly every aspect of their storm-tossed voyage. His account of their voyage is so full of detail, that many authorities site this chapter as one of the most informative sources available on ancient sea travel of that time. At some points along the way you may even find yourself becoming sea sick, as Luke describes the ship going up and down in the sea. In the events recorded by Luke we can find a number of allegories to the storms of our life.

The storm we will journey through had those within its grips frightened, uncertain, desperate, and hopeless. Sound familiar? Life's storms can do that at times. Beneath the darkness of their clouds and in the fierceness of their winds, even the strongest can become weak and fearful.

Perhaps somewhere on this journey you may recognize yourself in a storm you are currently experiencing. This voyage may even provide answers for some of the questions you have been asking in regards to life's difficult weather.

If you are not going through a storm at this time, be thankful and prepare yourself. As the title of this book suggests, it is not *if* the storms of life come... it is more a matter of *when*! They are an unfortunate fact of life. They will come. So hold on tight... There is some rough weather ahead!

John Buttrey
Anaheim, California 1998

1

When Troubles Come

In the day of my trouble
I will call upon You,
For You will answer me.
Psalm 86:7

I t is amazing how fast the weather of life can change. One minute we are smiling and enjoying life and those around us, unaware of any approaching storm... and the next, we are crying and concerned about life and possibly those we love. Often without warning, the storms of life arrive. Clear skies can become dark and cloudy in a very short time. How quickly the sun can disappear and the warm weather turn bitterly cold and difficult.

Job, the Patriarch of old, knew this very well. In one day, he lost his family and most of his possessions. It all happened so suddenly and without any warning. One by one messengers arrived to inform Job of disaster after disaster. And before each messenger could finish his report, another would arrive with even more bad news. Notice how the sacred record recounts this sudden and devastating storm.

> *A messenger came to Job and said, "The oxen were plowing and the donkeys feeding beside them, and the Sabeans attacked and took them. They also slew the servants with the edge of the sword, and I alone have escaped to tell you."*

While he was still speaking...

Another also came and said, "The fire of God fell from heaven and burned up the sheep and the servants and consumed them, and I alone have escaped to tell you."

While he was still speaking...

Another also came and said, "The Chaldeans formed three bands and made a raid on the camels and took them and slew the servants with the edge of the sword; and I alone have escaped to tell you."

While he was still speaking...

Another also came and said, "Your sons and your daughters were eating and drinking wine in their oldest brother's house, and behold, a great wind came from across the wilderness and struck the four corners of the house, and it fell on the young people and they died, and I alone have escaped to you."
Job 1:14-19 (NASB)

And as if all of that wasn't difficult enough to cope with, a short time later Job found himself covered in boils and lying in a pile of ashes. He is left like many of us from time to time, to deal with the aftermath of a destructive storm. A storm he never saw coming.

I have always found it interesting that when Job's friends came to comfort him, upon seeing the degree of the storm's toll, they sat for seven days and seven nights without saying a word.

The damage incurred from some storms can often leave the most well-intentioned encouragers speechless. Considering Job's situation at the time, what could they say? *"Everything is going to be ok!"*

Have you ever had someone tell you that during a difficult time? Have you ever said that yourself to someone? It sounds so comforting. The problem is they do not know that everything is going to be ok, and neither do you. Things may just get worse before they get better. That may sound negative, but unfortunately it is the truth. Nobody wants to be given false hope. That will only lead to more disappointment.

In my own life

How quickly things in life can change. With one phone call your world is thrown upside down. Confidence turns to confusion... happiness to sorrow... peace to chaos... clear skies become cloudy... and the weather of life becomes dark and stormy.

The weather of life changed very quickly for me in June of 1983. It was a time when everything in life seemed to be going great. My wife and I had been married for almost a year; we were expecting our first child; work was going well; we had purchased our first home; we had money in the bank; everything was great... So we thought. Little did we know that a storm was on its way. In fact, it had been brewing for some time. And the clear skies of life that we had been so accustomed to would soon begin growing dark with clouds. Within a week so much in life would change for us, and never quite be the same.

On Saturday June 18th the music band that my brother and I had put together, performed our annual backyard concert for our friends and a few neighbors. Aside from a few missed notes the concert was a tremendous success. The concert, as usual, was held in the backyard of my parent's home. Normally, the loud music drove them away, out to dinner or shopping for the evening. However, this time my mother stayed back in their bedroom during the evening's events because she was feeling sick. No one realized at the time just how sick she really was.

The day after the concert, my wife and I stopped by my parent's home to visit my mother, and to do some final cleaning up from the previous evening. We all had dinner together and enjoyed some good conversation. Mom seemed to be feeling better, although at the time, I was more ecstatic about the concert. But Monday would quickly change my feelings and interests. That's when the phone call came... *"We had to take mom to the hospital."*

For most of that week, as she lay in that hospital bed, she remained comatose. She had battled with cancer before, but never to this extent. We were all shocked, but confident she would pull through just as always. After all, she was young... only in her late forties... she still had children at home... everything would be fine. That's what we all kept telling ourselves. It was what we all believed.

The conversations in the waiting room that week were mostly optimistic. Oftentimes they were directed towards other areas of life. Things like, sports scores, television programs, or the political news of the day. A purposeful but unsuccessful attempt to avoid thinking about the current situation.

On Saturday morning she left this life. Her week-long battle eventually gave way to death, and she was gone. All that remained of the one I knew as *"Mom,"* were all kinds of precious and wonderful memories. She left behind a loving husband, four children, many friends, lots of brothers and sisters in Christ, and one unborn granddaughter.

That was only one of many *"storms"* which have come my way. I am sure you have experienced, or are currently experiencing, your own. Storms no doubt greater than those life has sent my way. One thing to know for sure about the storms of life... they are no respecter of persons! They hit everyone.

Life's storms do not always involve the loss of loved ones. At times it may be the loss of a job... a time of depression... marital discord... conflict with family... discovering your spouse has been unfaithful... a trying and difficult illness... financial struggles. The storms of life can take the form of any number of different circumstances and events. Difficult circumstances which can affect people in many different ways. What is a storm for one person, may only be a passing gentle breeze for another. Whether a passing gentle breeze or a torrent of clouds and rain, storms of various degrees of intensity do come. Some will prove very severe and difficult to weather... others merely inconvenient nuisances.

An apostle named Paul

When troubles come, they often come quickly. The apostle Paul certainly found this to be true. He knew how quickly the weather of life could change. Traveling from city to city and spreading the gospel, Paul experienced all kinds of difficulties and sudden changes of events. Angry groups of people from cities where he had been would follow him and turn his audiences against him. He was stoned and left for dead, beaten, forced out of town, and falsely accused. Paul knew all about troubles. Yet through it all, Paul kept going. He refused to quit.

One trip in particular would usher Paul into some very difficult and trying circumstances, the kind of times Paul was accustomed to. It was a trip into Jerusalem that would lead to his arrest and ultimately to a storm-filled voyage to Italy, where he was to go on trial for preaching the gospel.

Prior to making this trip, a prophet named Agabus came down from Judea, warning Paul about his destination. Agabus took Paul's belt, bound his own hands and feet and warned Paul, saying, *"This is what will happen to you in Jerusalem."* When those present heard those words, they pleaded with Paul not to go. Yet despite their earnest pleadings, Paul, undaunted, would proceed as planned to Jerusalem.

Trouble in Jerusalem

Paul was determined to go to Jerusalem. He had seen and dealt with trouble before. What Agabus warned him about was nothing too unusual for Paul. So, off to Jerusalem he went. It is there that things really began to get out of control, although the trip seemed to start off very well, Luke records in Acts 21:17, *"The brethren received us gladly."* How quickly things would change!

An angry group of people from some surrounding areas showed up and started turning the people against Paul. This led to a near riot and Paul being beaten by the people. After being rescued by some Roman soldiers, Paul asks permission to address the angry crowd of people, which he is allowed to do. However, that only seems to make matters worse. To quiet the crowd, he is taken into custody, and was about to be beaten again. This time by the soldiers, until they discovered that he was a Roman citizen. Once that information is learned, they cease from their intended actions, knowing that it was unlawful for them to scourge Paul without a proper trial.

As we said earlier, Paul was no stranger to trouble. He found more than his share of it in Jerusalem. The fact that he was a

Roman citizen may have helped to cease the scourging he was about to receive, but it did not get him out of jail. It did not take away his troubles. In fact, more were on the way. A series of trials, a plot by the Jews to kill him, and a trip to Rome full of stormy weather still awaited Paul. The bad weather of life had arrived, and it was going to hang around for awhile.

Faith, hope, and love

How quickly things can change. From *"the brethren received us gladly"* to... angry people, arrest, scourging, and people trying to kill him. Life for Paul had definitely changed... but through it all, his faith, hope, and love for God had not wavered. In his Roman letter, Paul wrote...

> *And not only this, but we also exult in our tribulations, knowing that tribulation brings about perseverance; and perseverance, proven character; and proven character, hope;*
> Romans 5:3-4 (NASB)

Paul in that text says we should exult in tribulations. Is that really possible? How can one possibly *"exult in tribulations"*? How can one glory when the storms of life come their way? How? Paul tells us in that verse. In essence he says, *"All these troubles, trials, and storms make my **faith** stronger. They help me to remember my **hope**. And with hope, I am reminded of God's great **love** for me."* How important! Faith, hope and love.

The storms of life will quickly challenge your faith. They will try and blind you from your hope. They have even been known to cause some to question God's love for them. *"How could God do this to me? I thought He loved me?"*

Understand something, no matter what you may be going through... no matter how severe the storm... God does love you! Notice how Paul (in the above referenced scripture) continues speaking of God's love for you.

> *For while we* (**you**) *were still helpless, at the right time Christ died for* (**you**) *the ungodly. For one will hardly die for a righteous man; though perhaps for the good man someone would dare even to die. But God demonstrates His own love toward us* (**you**), *in that while we were yet sinners, Christ died for us* (**you**).
>
> Romans 5:6-8 (NASB)[2]

Paul says even though you were weak... even though you were ungodly... even though you had sinned... God still loves you! He loves you so much He sent His Son to die for you. Isn't that amazing? If God loves you in those conditions, surely He loves you during the storms of life! Understanding God's incredible love for you is the key for maintaining faith, hope, and love in the midst of life's often devastating weather.

When life seems to be caving in all around you; when you are getting drenched in a downpour of trouble; remember God loves you! Let that thought keep your faith strong and secure and your hope alive and confident. How important indeed are faith, hope, and love.

- A **faith** that knows God is still in control.
- A **hope** that is confident in God's promises.
- A **love** that inspires and motivates.
- A **faith** that believes God is still with me.
- A **hope** that is confident God has not abandoned me.
- A **love** that feels His tender compassion and care.

Listen to the strong faith and confident hope of a man firmly secure in his mind that God loved him. These are thought to be some of the last words from the pen of Paul. At the time, he was writing from the tight quarters of a cold and damp Roman dungeon; and in his mind, was the knowledge that his death could be any time soon. Yet notice the confidence with which he writes.

> *For I am already being poured out as a drink offering, and the time of my departure has come. I have fought the good fight, I have finished the course, I have kept the faith; in the future there is laid up for me the crown of righteousness, which the Lord, the righteous Judge, will award to me on that day, and not only to me, but also to all who have loved His appearing.*
> 2 Timothy 4:6-8 (NASB)

Isn't that amazing? That kind of attitude is the result of faith, hope, and love. Despite all the abundant and frequent troubles he had experienced, Paul still expresses his confidence that God would provide what He had promised. Paul said it well even earlier in the same letter:

> *For this reason I also suffer these things, but I am not ashamed; for I know whom I have believed and I am convinced that He is able to guard what I have entrusted to Him until that day.*
> 2 Timothy 1:12 (NASB)

That is a strong faith! That is a confident hope! Those are the words of a man who knew God loved him. Paul was convinced of his eternal reward. For Paul, there was no doubt. He knew, his eternal reward was as sure as his impending death. His strong and confident attitude was the result of faith, hope, and love.

It would be this same kind of faith, hope and love that would help get Paul through one of the most challenging and dangerous voyages of his life. A storm-tossed journey to Rome to stand trial for the events in Jerusalem for which he was arrested. When troubles come, they often come quickly. And, for Paul, more were on their way.

2

Setting Sail

Trust in the Lord with all your heart,
And lean not on your own understanding;
In all your ways acknowledge Him,
And He shall direct your paths.
Proverbs 3:5-6

S etting sail. Those words speak of embarking. Hoisting up the anchor, raising the sails, and letting the driving force of the wind propel us off to our desired destination. There we are, with a refreshing sense of freedom, heading out on a course to new horizons and exciting adventures. With chart and compass nearby, and our hands on the wheel, we are on our way. Setting sail, we look forward with great expectation and anxious anticipation to arrival at our planned destination. But sometimes, reaching that destination can be quite interesting, at times even difficult.

When setting sail on a journey only a few of us ever anticipate any serious problems. We expect the waters to be smooth. We expect to arrive safely. We expect good weather. But, oftentimes our expectations do not meet with reality. On occasion, and unexpectedly, the storm clouds come. With them come difficulties and challenges. The navigating becomes tedious and sometimes seemingly impossible. Winds that at one time were in our favor, now blow hard against us. Staying on course requires constant and tireless attention, and lots of careful maneuvering.

People set sail almost every day on journeys that prove more difficult than expected or imagined. The smooth voyages they had hoped for turn into constant battles for survival.

- Setting sail on a business venture, but having the excitement threatened by rough waters.
- Setting sail in a new relationship, a *"can't miss"*, yet in time, it appears doomed for shipwreck.
- Setting sail in a career where the future that looked so bright is darkened by looming clouds.

Obviously, this is not the case for everyone. Many times we find the results of our journeys far exceed our expectations... but not always. We all need to understand that oftentimes life can hold the unexpected. And, the unexpected in life is not always good. In fact, sometimes life's unexpected circumstances can be very frightening and extremely discouraging.

Ask the parents, who never expected their family to be devastated by the unexpected loss of a child. Ask the woman, who has unexpectedly become a widow. Ask the family, who has had their home destroyed by fire. Ask the husband, who watches helplessly as his wife lay in a hospital bed with tubes and wires connecting her to all kinds of strange machinery. All of these situations, and others like them are an often-unexpected fact of life. They are the unexpected storms of life.

The beginnings of a doomed voyage

In the twenty-seventh chapter of the book of Acts, we find a group of men setting sail on a very long and difficult journey. No doubt they were not expecting the kind of bad weather they experienced, for had they known what was in store, it is likely they would have never set sail.

On board the ship with these men was the apostle Paul, heading for Rome to stand trial. As we have already noted, Paul was arrested in Jerusalem for preaching about Jesus Christ. From Jerusalem, he was transferred to Caesarea because of a plot to kill him. Now, because of an appeal Paul himself had made, he would be brought to Rome to stand trial.

Paul had earlier made the statement, *"I must see Rome."*[3] I wonder if he realized at that time just how he would get there? Arrested, scourged, Jewish trials, Roman trials, imprisonment, the troubles, which began for Paul in Jerusalem, were about to continue. And as if the weather of life weren't stormy enough, Paul is about to head out into a real storm, setting sail on a voyage that will end in shipwreck!

> *And when it was decided that we should sail to Italy, they delivered Paul and some other prisoners to one named Julius, a centurion of the Augustan Regiment. So, entering a ship of Adramyttium, we put to sea, meaning to sail along the coasts of Asia. Aristarchus, a Macedonian of Thessalonica, was with us. And the next day we landed at Sidon. And Julius treated Paul kindly and gave him liberty to go to his friends and receive care.*

Acts 27:1-3

The journey to Rome begins. They set sail and make their first stop at a place called Sidon. It is here the centurion guarding Paul shows much confidence and trust in him by allowing him parole. His doing so says a lot about the character of Paul. Even though he was a prisoner, the centurion guarding him knew he could trust him. With his granted liberty, Paul leaves the ship and goes ashore. It is there, on shore, that he visits and receives care from some of his friends.

What a joy that must have been for Paul! These are friends that he had perhaps not seen for some time. Good friends can often make our journey through this life so much more enjoyable, especially during those times of stormy weather. When the weather of life gets a little too cold, they provide much needed comfort and warmth. They give us words of encouragement and support, and at times, a shoulder to cry on and a hand we can hold. How comforting the time with his friends must have been for Paul. However, the time to set sail again quickly arrived, forcing Paul to say good-bye, so he could return to the ship.

Back at sea, the crew of the ship soon find things are not going to be exactly as they had planned. The smooth trip they had hoped for is starting to get a little rough.

> *When we had put to sea from there, we sailed under the shelter of Cyprus, because the winds were contrary.*
>
> Acts 27:4

"The winds were contrary." Isn't that just like life at times? *"Contrary."* Those are the times when you usually find yourself experiencing more than your share of failure. Times when you wonder, *"What's going on?"* When life starts getting *"contrary"* for us, it is often a sign that difficult weather has arrived. A sign a storm may be present or on its way. For the men on board this ship, the winds of the storm are already beginning to blow. Little did they know, it had only just begun.

> *And when we had sailed over the sea which is off Cilicia and Pamphylia, we came to Myra, a city of Lycia. There the centurion found an Alexandrian ship sailing to Italy, and he put us on board.*
>
> Acts 27:5-6

Changing Ships

Because things were not going as they had expected, they make another stop. This time the stop is at Myra. It is here at Myra, that the centurion changes ships. He finds another ship bound for Italy and he decides to move his prisoners on board.

The ship they were transferring to may have appealed to the centurion, for it was apparently quite large, perhaps much larger than the previous vessel. Later we find that with crew and passengers this ship held two hundred and seventy-six passengers and a cargo of wheat. Luke tells us it was an Alexandrian ship. Meaning it was from Alexandria in Northern Africa. These ships were used for carrying wheat from Egypt to Italy. The fact that this ship was at Myra, may indicate it was driven out of its normal route by the adverse winds of a storm. If that be the case, the centurion is transferring his prisoners to a ship already off course and experiencing difficulty!

Perhaps the centurion thought changing ships would make the sailing to Italy smoother. That this other vessel would fare better against the strength of the storm. However, he would quickly become aware of the error of his thinking. Changing ships would not quell the storm... it never does.

How many people today try that same kind of thing when the storms of life come? They *"change ships"* so to speak, thinking that will make things better. By changing ships, they think they will find peace of mind... all their problems will be solved. By changing ships, they just know they will find real happiness. However, sometimes these other *"ships"* may already be off course and in trouble themselves!

- "I'll change careers! That will help."
- "I'll move... I just know the grass is greener over there!"
- "I'll have an affair... that will spice things up."

Rather than facing the problem of life's bad weather, they ignore it and try moving on to something different. Yet, despite the changes, the problem still remains! *"Changing ships"* will not take away the storm! It does not solve the problem they may be facing. Unfortunately, many find this out after they have changed ships and, oftentimes, direction. The centurion certainly found this to be true.

> *When we had sailed slowly many days, and arrived with difficulty off Cnidus, the wind not permitting us to proceed, we sailed under the shelter of Crete off Salmone. Passing it with difficulty, we came to a place called Fair Havens, near the city of Lasea.*
> Acts 27:7-8

Take a look at some of the descriptions of their journey so far...

- The winds were contrary.
- Sailed slowly for many days.
- Arrived with difficulty.
- The wind did not permit us.
- Passing it with difficulty.

This is not your average cruise on the Mediterranean! Like life at times, it was a constant struggle. Everything seemed to be working against them. It was going slow. It was hard, frustrating, and difficult. You have probably known times like that in your life. Perhaps it describes your life right now.

- Those times when everything you do seems to be wrong.
- When nothing seems to be going right.
- When you can't seem to make the right decisions.
- When life seemingly has you in its cross hairs and is taking shots at you, and you find yourself constantly running for shelter.

These are times most of us never expect, but at some point, usually find ourselves having to carefully navigate through. For the crew and passengers on board the ship, this storm had them in its sights, and it was not about to let up. It had them sailing slowly for many days and arriving with difficulty. With such a constant struggle, it seems ironic that they would make a stop at a place called *"Fair Havens."* With a name like that, it would seem like a nice place to visit and spend some time. And, needing a break from the weather, they decided to do so. However, they apparently spend too much time in Fair Havens.

> *Now when much time had been spent, and sailing was now dangerous because the Fast was already over, Paul advised them,*
> Acts 27: 9

Storm Warnings

A considerable amount of time had been spent in Fair Havens. Maybe they were waiting for better weather, but things were not clearing up. That's usually the way it is with storms. You never seem to know just how long they will last. Storms seem to have their own time schedule. Just when you think things are beginning to clear up, life's weather may sometimes begin to get darker... cloudier... and difficult.

21

When Luke tells us the fast was over, it is likely that he has reference to the Jewish Day of Atonement, which would indicate that the events taking place here were occurring sometime near the first part of October. That might not sound like an important detail; but when one understands that sailing on the Mediterranean was not considered safe for ships of that time from about early September to March; it then becomes very significant. In fact, it probably explains why he writes, *"sailing was now dangerous."* It also explains Paul's warning to the men of the ship.

> *Paul advised them, saying, "Men, I perceive that this voyage will end with disaster and much loss, not only of the cargo and ship, but also our lives."*
> Acts 27: 9b, 10

Paul here sounds very much like the preacher he was. He is trying with his words and actions to warn others about the dangers of a particular course of life. He tries to warn these men about the threatening doom of this storm. He issues a serious storm warning. *"Men, I perceive that this voyage will end with disaster and much loss, not only of the cargo and ship, but also our lives."* However, just like with preachers and others who try to warn people about the obvious consequences of their choice of direction, they refuse to listen.

> *Nevertheless the centurion was more persuaded by the helmsman and the owner of the ship than by the things spoken by Paul. And because the harbor was not suitable to winter in, the majority advised to set sail from there also, if by any means they could*

> reach Phoenix, a harbor of Crete opening toward the
> southwest and northwest, and winter there.
> Acts 27:11-12

I can just hear the helmsman of this ship. *"I've been sailing these waters for years." "Are you going to listen to a Jewish prisoner or me?" "I know what I'm doing!" "Don't tell me what to do!"* Any of that sound familiar?

Pride can be a very dangerous thing. It prevents us from really listening to what others may have to say. There was no way the helmsman was going to listen to the storm warnings of a Jewish prisoner. As a result, he would find himself in some very perilous waters. Solomon warned about the dangers of pride in the familiar proverb,

> *Pride goes before destruction,*
> *And a haughty spirit before a fall.*
> Proverbs 16:18

Pride blinds us to what others have to offer. Pride says, *"I don't need their help." "I don't need their advice." "I don't need anybody." "I can handle it."*

There are times when people offer us advise on avoiding storms; or how to get through them. But oftentimes, in our pride, we won't listen. As a result, at times, we incur unnecessary disaster and loss. The helmsman of this ship, and his crew, were about to find this out the hard way.

Avoiding unnecessary shipwreck

We have already discussed how life can sometimes hold the unexpected. At times, journeys intended to lead to success and prosperity, end unexpectedly in (what we could call) shipwreck.

There are times when these disasters can not be avoided, they are an unfortunate part of life. However, there are some ways to possibly avoid *some* of our shipwrecks in this life. Those we later, oftentimes learn, *could have* been prevented.

If you think about some of the ways actual sea-worthy ships suffer shipwreck; I believe you will see some ways we can keep on sailing through many of our journeys in life; avoiding shipwreck. Why do shipwrecks occur?

- **Poor navigation skills:** Not knowing how you are going to get where you want to be in life. Not knowing where you are going. If you have no direction in life, no planned course or destination, you are possibly heading for disaster.

- **Traveling through unfamiliar waters:** Getting involved in things you really should not be involved in. Going to places you know you should not be. Be aware of your surroundings and company.

- **Ignoring wise counsel:** Much like the men of this ship we have been discussing, ignoring wise counsel is scoffing at the advice of others with perhaps more experience and knowledge in a particular area. It is ignoring, because of pride, sound and factual information.

- **Bad weather:** It is a part of life, when it comes, hold on tight and keep your course. Be alert to the changing weather of life and recognize it when it comes. Through good or bad, clouds or sunshine, remember the importance of faith, hope, and love.

3

A Place To Winter In

For You have been
a strength to the poor,
A strength to the needy in his distress,
A refuge from the storm,
Isaiah 25:4a

There is such a beautiful variety of sights and sounds in the changing seasons of the year. God has designed nature with its own incredible clock. With such remarkable precision and accuracy its invisible hands slowly tick, signaling seasonal times of change throughout the year. Each season comes with amazing regularity and striking contrasts. The changing of each season brings changes in color and appearance, sometimes subtle, sometimes extreme.

Spring brings with it the freshness of its air. The freshness of spring seems to breed new life in all of nature. It is seen blossoming nearly everywhere you look. Then comes the summer with its clear and sunny skies. The warm weather of summer beckons a time of freedom and running barefoot. Fall brings its time of maturing change. The changing of its colors alter the appearance of nature's landscape. And then comes the winter, and with it the beauty of the snow capped mountains and the briskness of its cooler temperatures.

Yet, as beautiful as all of the different seasons are, changes in the seasons bring changes in the weather. Weather changes that can sometimes bring difficulties, especially in the winter. Wintertime can be a difficult time for travel. Its severe cold and icy temperatures can make just about any kind of travel burdensome.

Paul expressed his knowledge of the cold and sometimes difficult weather of winter, as he wrote to Timothy from his Roman dungeon, towards the end of life. *"Make every effort to come before winter."*[4] He told Timothy to bring with him the cloak that he had left in Troas.[5] Paul knew the winter temperatures of the dungeon would require some means of keeping warm. He was preparing for winter.

Winter travel was something the men of this ship were apparently very much concerned about. They knew the dangers of winter sailing on the Mediterranean Sea.

> *Nevertheless the centurion was more persuaded by the helmsman and the owner of the ship than by the things spoken by Paul. And because the harbor was not suitable to winter in, the majority advised to set sail from there also, if by any means they could reach Phoenix, a harbor of Crete opening toward the southwest and northwest, and winter there.*
>
> Acts 27:11-12

They were searching for a place to spend the winter. A place of shelter where they could wait out the storm and its violent force. A place of protection from the severity of the rough weather they were experiencing. A place where they could dock the ship until the sailing conditions would be better and the seas more calm. A place they could winter in. Isn't that what we are all looking for when life's storms come? A place that we can "winter" from the storm?

- A place of shelter and rest.
- A place of protection and warmth.
- A place to wait out the severe weather.

Having a good place to winter in is so important when the seasons of life change and its weather becomes hard and severe. Just as sure as nature will bring changes in the seasons, life is full of its own changes in climate. Solomon described life's changing seasons so well in the familiar words of Ecclesiastes chapter three...

To every thing there is a season,
And a time to every purpose under the heaven:
A time to be born, and a time to die;
A time to plant, and a time to pluck up that which is planted;
A time to kill, and a time to heal;
A time to break down, and a time to build up;
A time to weep, and a time to laugh;
A time to mourn, and a time to dance;
A time to cast away stones, and a time to gather stones
together;
A time to embrace, and a time to refrain from embracing;
A time to get, and a time to lose;
A time to keep, and a time to cast away;
A time to rend, and a time to sew;
A time to keep silence, and a time to speak;
A time to love, and a time to hate;
A time of war, and a time of peace.
Ecclesiastes 3:1-8 (KJV)

With all the many different times and seasons of life, some of which will prove to be difficult and stormy, it is important to have a place to winter in. But where does one find such a place?

At times, it may be in the arms of a family member or close friend. Friends and family are often a safe harbor for life's storms. They provide a special kind of warmth when life's weather changes and becomes too cold and difficult. The company and care of friends and family can be like a giant umbrella, shielding us from the onslaught of life's downpours. They shelter us with their love and concern. They comfort us with their words of encouragement and hope, providing security when the moorings, which keep us stable, are in danger of snapping.

Yet, as special as friends and family are in providing warmth and shelter during our difficult seasons, the best place for us to find shelter during the storms of life is with God. The prophet Isaiah described the shelter God can provide us, when he wrote,

> *For You have been a strength to the poor, A strength*
> *to the needy in his distress, A refuge from the storm,*
> *A shade from the heat; For the blast of the terrible*
> *ones is as a storm against the wall.*
> Isaiah 25:4

Look closely at all the wonderful ways Isaiah says God provides protection for us during life's stormy weather.

- A strength... *When we are weak.*
- A refuge... *When we need shelter.*
- A shade... *When the weather is severe.*

Isaiah was not alone in his knowledge of God's ability to help us in weathering the storms of life. The great king, David, also understood the shelter God can provide. During his life, David experienced many storms. As a young man, there was the jealousy of King Saul. Later, he would experience various family problems. Caving in to lust led to the storm of an illicit affair and the death of a baby. There was the death of a rebellious son. And, times he would have to deal with the guilt of his own sins.

30

Yet, when life's storms hit, David had a place of refuge. A harbor safe and warm. It was with God. Enjoying the protection and comfort found in Him. Listen to how David described his divine place of shelter.

> *Hear my cry, O God; Give heed to my prayer. From the end of the earth I call to You when my heart is faint; Lead me to the rock that is higher than I. For You have been a refuge for me, A tower of strength against the enemy. Let me dwell in Your tent forever; Let me take refuge in the shelter of Your wings.*
>
> Psalm 61:1-4 (NASB)

Take a closer look at some of the descriptions David uses as he tells us about this wonderful place for wintering that we too can go to find safety and comfort.

- A rock...   *When we need a sure foundation.*
- A tower of strength...   *When we need a place of defense.*
- A tent...   *When we're seeking God's presence.*
- A refuge...   *When we need a place of protection.*

Considering all these wonderful benefits Isaiah and David have described, doesn't God sound like a wonderful place to winter? God is the best place for us to turn when life's seasons become hard and difficult. He provides a comforting refuge available for all His children... we just need to turn to Him! Isaiah knew where to turn. David looked to God for the protection and shelter he needed. Let us do the same. The old hymn writer of years ago, Isaac Watts, put it like this...

O God, our help in ages past,
Our Hope for years to come,
Our shelter from the stormy blast,
And our eternal home.
Under the shadow of Thy throne,
Still may we dwell secure,
Sufficient is Thine arm alone, And our defense is sure.[6]

What a wonderful place of shelter, rest, and comfort there is to be found with God. A place to build ourselves up for facing the re-occurring storms of life. Whether it's spending time reading His Word, kneeling in prayer, or in the company of our brothers and sisters in Christ, God provides us a wonderful place, not only to winter in, but also to spend all the seasons of our lives.

Though the winter may seem long, eventually that precision-filled clock will signal a change in the seasons. When the winter of life finally ends, and the weather becomes fair, enjoy it! Rejoice and give God the glory.

My beloved spoke, and said to me:
"Rise up, my love, my fair one, And come away.
For lo, the winter is past, The rain is over and gone.
Song of Solomon 2:10-11

4

In The Storm

---

*But when he saw
that the wind was boisterous,
he was afraid;
and beginning to sink
he cried out, saying,
"Lord, save me!"*
Matthew 14:30

As the owner of the ship, the helmsman, and the centurion, discussed whether or not to set sail, Paul tried to warn them about the dangers of the impending weather. Yet, despite his warnings, they decided to go ahead and set sail anyway, hoping to find a place to spend the winter. After all, the weather appeared to be getting better and the wind did not seem to be blowing as hard. However, storms can often be deceiving. They would soon find they should have listened to Paul.

> *When the south wind blew softly, supposing that they had obtained their desire, putting out to sea, they sailed close by Crete. But not long after, a tempestuous head wind arose, called Euroclydon.*
> Acts 27:13-14

As they set sail again, the weather appeared to be very safe. Luke says, *"The south wind blew softly."* In other words, the wind wasn't blowing that hard. The weather appeared to be fine... ideal for sailing. But, after venturing out into the sea the storm really hits!

At times, the strength and intensity of storms can be very deceiving. Often, even the calmest of weather can turn dark, ominous, and threatening in a very short time. In fact, it was not long after they set sail that a violent wind arose against them; a wind full of strength and power. It was so strong and powerful that the people of that day and time knew it by a special name... Euroclydon. The Euroclydon would create mighty storms with huge waves and powerful winds. They now find themselves in the midst of a serious and life-threatening storm. One that is really pounding on them. The rrrumble of thunder, flashes of lightning, and howling winds, are clear evidence of the fact, that they are in the thick of some very dangerous and terrorizing weather.

> *So when the ship was caught, and could not head*
> *into the wind, we let her drive.*
> Acts 27:15

Notice how Luke describes their perilous predicament, *"The ship was caught!"* In other words, it was out of their control and in the grips of the storm. There was nothing they could do. Luke says because of the strength of the storm, *"We let her drive."*

They were powerless compared to the strength of this storm. The storm would decide which direction they would take. The storm would decide how fast or slow they would go. The strong winds and restless seas were demanding their submissive obedience. Stating in no uncertain terms, as the clouds boldly rumbled with the frightening sounds of thunder, *"You are no longer in control, I am!"*

Have you ever felt that way when life's storms have lashed at you? Like everything is completely out of control? There are those times in life when we feel powerless to make any changes in direction. Much like a ship that is caught. The only thing we can really do is... *"Let her drive."* And, turn to God in prayer.

The winds from storms can blow us away at times. They make us weak. They knock us down. They blow us off course. I think that at that point it is easy to just want to quit. We give up fighting. We quit trying. Life knocks us down and we stay there. The men on board this ship were close to that point.

> *And running under the shelter of an island called Clauda, we secured the skiff with difficulty.*
>
> Acts 27:16

The *"skiff"* was a little boat they would use to sail from the main ship; to go to shore or to another ship. What we today would know as a rowboat or lifeboat. Considering the intensity of this storm, the skiff was something of great value to these men. That's why they went to such great lengths to secure it.

Just imagine these terrified and rain-soaked men pulling and straining to get this little boat on board. All the while the ship is bouncing up and down from the huge waves. Luke says that they secured it with difficulty. They were no doubt determined to get the skiff on board because it might possibly be their only hope of escape should the main ship begin to sink.

Everyone would like a way of escape when storms come. A skiff we can jump into in case of emergency. Something we can hold onto when everything around us seems to be sinking. A source and means of rescue when doom seems imminent. Some ray of hope when everything else seems hopeless.

> *When they had taken it on board, they used cables to undergird the ship; and fearing lest they should run aground on the Syrtis Sands, they struck sail and so were driven.*
>
> Acts 27:17

Undergirding

After getting the skiff on board, Luke says they used cables to undergird the ship. Undergirding a ship was a process whereby they would pass cables under and around the exterior of the ship, binding it together to try to keep it from being torn apart in bad weather. It was a means of keeping it strong and secure.

What a beautiful picture of a need we all have at different times in life... those times when we need some undergirding. When cables of support are needed to keep us from coming apart during life's storms. When our ship is starting to leak because of the adverse weather of life, and we find ourselves doing everything we can to stay afloat. When times like that occur (and they will), sound a cry for help, it is time for some undergirding. Undergirding will give us the strength and support we need for the difficult waters we often must navigate through.

The undergirding cables for us might be many different things. There are the cables of God's word and the strength and comfort found within its pages. On other occasions it may be the support found in our Christian family. In fact, that is one of the reasons we have such a wonderful spiritual family. To provide us loving and caring brethren to pass the cables of faith and hope around us, giving us strength and security when we are being tossed about. To equip us with caring and compassionate friends who can keep us from falling to pieces and breaking apart.

Paul described the importance of the family relationship we share in Christ as a body that is joined and knit together. He wrote to church at Ephesus...

*From whom the whole body, being **fitted and held together** by that which every joint supplies, according to the proper working of each individual*

part, causes the growth of the body for the building up of itself in love.[7]
Ephesians 4:16 (NASB)

It is with God and our Christian family that we can find the spiritual and emotional undergirding we so often need. When I think of what this spiritual family can do for us, I can not help but think of the old hymn...

Blest be the TIE *that* BINDS, *our hearts in Christian love...*

This love and special tie we share as brothers and sisters in Christ has been the binding undergirding cables of security and strength for many throughout the years. Just knowing there are others who are near. Being aware that there are others who are willing to help, is a very secure feeling, an undergirding for getting through life. Blest indeed is the tie that binds!

I want you to try to picture this scene of these men working together, in the storm, to undergird this ship. They are yelling at each other...

"Send it over!" "Here it comes!"
"One more time!" "I've got it!"
"Together, pull!" "We did it!"

Just like with us today, especially during the difficult times of life, it would take all of them working together, in the midst of the storm, to undergird and make this ship secure.

What a scene! This is real high-seas adventure! The kind of drama great adventure movies and books are made from. These storm-weary men are getting splashed with waves. They're being tossed back and forth as the large swells of the sea cause the ship to rise and fall at the whim of the storm. Rocking back and forth, they are holding as tightly as they can, to whatever they can find, to avoid falling overboard. The wood of the ship is creaking; perhaps even starting to leak in spots as the raindrops pile drive mercilessly against the ship. The wind is howling, blowing salt water and rain beating against their faces. It is cold, damp, and dark. To understand just how intense this scene and storm really was, Luke tells us...

> *And because we were exceedingly tempest-tossed, the next day they lightened the ship. On the third day we threw the ship's tackle overboard with our own hands. Now when neither sun nor stars appeared for many days, and no small tempest beat on us, all hope that we would be saved was finally given up.*
> Acts 27:18-20

"Exceedingly tempest-tossed..." *"No small tempest beat on us..."* The fierceness of the storm, the constant pounding of the waves, the lack of light (no sun or stars for many days), the state of constant darkness, all of this brought them to a point of hopelessness. Notice the line from Luke's *"journal"* of the voyage... *"All hope that we would be saved was finally given up."*

Storms have a way of doing that. When there doesn't seem to be any end in sight... when the pounding and pressure won't let up... when there doesn't seem to be any light... we lose hope. And without hope, we give up.

The men on board the ship were ready to give up. They'd had enough. Day in and day out... all night long... it just would not stop. They were tired, exhausted, frustrated, and hungry.

In a desperate attempt to survive, they lightened the ship by throwing some of the ship's cargo and tackle overboard. At the same time, each of the crewmembers and passengers must have wondered if, and when, they might be thrown overboard by the storm into the raging sea!

> *But after long abstinence from food, then Paul stood in the midst of them and said, "Men, you should have listened to me, and not have sailed from Crete, and incurred this disaster and loss.*
> Acts 27:21

I love that verse! *"Men, you should have listened to me!"* Remember Paul's warning to them about setting sail earlier? He tried to warn them to wait, but they ignored him. As a result, they now found themselves in serious danger.

When Storms Come

5

A Friend Like Luke

A friend loves at all times,
And a brother is born for adversity.
Proverbs 17:17

L et's take a short break from the storm we've been traveling through. The weather has been getting rough and treacherous, so let's talk for a moment about something very refreshing. Consider this chapter a place to winter in as we journey through the stormy weather we've been reading about.

We have been talking a lot about Paul thus far in our journey; but there is someone else we need to discuss. An individual who was right there in the midst of the downpour with Paul. One who was keeping track of everything that was happening, in a kind of journal. Recording with his pen, all of the events taking place on this rough voyage. That someone was Luke. What a special friend Luke was to Paul.

Luke doesn't mention his name in the text, but his presence on the journey is evident. Luke is the most widely recognized author of the book of Acts. His presence on this journey is seen in such statements as these…

- And when it was decided that **we** should sail to Italy,[8]
- So, entering a ship of Adramyttium, **we** put to sea, meaning to sail along the coasts of Asia. Aristarchus, a Macedonian of Thessalonica, was with **us**.[9]
- And the next day **we** landed at Sidon.[10]

Over and over again, Luke refers to himself and Paul, as *"we"* or *"us."* As far as this storm is concerned, Luke was right there in the middle of it. Experiencing along with Paul every drop of rain, every crack of the lightning, and every rock and creak of the ship. Good friends stick with us during the storms of life. They ride them out with us. Friends like Luke don't abandon us in difficult times.

This voyage was not the only storm of life that Luke had endured with Paul. I can picture Luke right alongside Paul during some of the events Paul described to the brethren at Corinth:[11] the beatings, the various perils, the hungering and thirsting, the cold and nakedness. It would take quite a good friend to stick close to Paul in those difficult times. Yet, Luke did. That's the kind of friend he was.

Towards the end of Paul's life, as he was facing certain death, chained in a Roman dungeon, and writing what was possibly his final letter, Luke was again right there with him. Faithful to the end, just as good friends always are. Paul in writing to another good friend, Timothy, makes mention of Luke's presence at that time.

> *Only Luke is with me. Get Mark and bring him with you, for he is useful to me for ministry.*
> 2 Timothy 4:11

That is such a beautiful verse. One that we often just read right through without a second thought. Don't do that! That verse says a lot about the character of Luke. *Only Luke is with me."* Later in that same text Paul wrote,

> *At my first defense no one stood with me, but all forsook me. May it not be charged against them.*
> 2 Timothy 4:16

All had forsaken Paul, all but Luke. How comforting it must have been to be able to write of Luke's company at that difficult time. I can just picture Paul as he writes those words, looking across at Luke with a smile, remembering all the good and bad times they had been through together.

Think of what it took for Luke to be present at that time. To stick close to Paul's side during some of those different storms of life. Think of that... and you'll see what a good friend is all about.

When we think of good friends in the Bible, perhaps most of us think of Jonathan and David. What a special friendship these two shared.

> *Now it came about when he had finished speaking to Saul, that the soul of Jonathan was knit to the soul of David, and Jonathan loved him as himself.*
> 1 Samuel 18:1 (NASB)

That's a close friend! That's what friendships are all about. *"Souls"* knit together. Close friends are bound together in soul, in heart, looking out for one another. They share the experiences of life together. Enjoying the good times, and holding on tight to each other when the tempests of life blow hard. That's the kind of friends Luke and Paul were... knit together in soul.

Do you have a friend or friends like that? Someone like Luke? Like Jonathan? Someone who is always there for you? A special friend with whom you have been through all kinds of weather, good and bad? If so, you know what a blessing and joy good friends can be.

Good friendships are special relationships that just seem to grow closer through years. How special and valuable are good friends. How important it is to know there is someone who you can count on to be there for you, no matter what the occasion or weather.

Solomon described the depth and beauty of certain friendships when he wrote...

A friend loves at all times, And a brother is born for adversity.
Proverbs 17:17

The idea of that proverb is that there are friends... and then there are *friends!* Those special friends who, at times, become closer to us than family. Sharing the experiences of life together, the trials, the troubles, the heartaches, the storms, brings people closer together.

A good friend will always be there for you. But if that friend sticks with you through the storms of life, he will become more than just a friend... he will become as a brother. That was Luke to Paul.

When trials are endured together, there is a closeness that develops between friends. A certain bond which is hard to break. Paul and Luke had that kind of friendship. They had a strong bond that could not be broken. Their special and close friendship found Luke right by Paul's side, no matter what, like a brother.

Chances are you can think of times in your life. Times when a good friend played a key role in your dealing with a particular difficulty. Times when, without the help of that friend or a group of friends, you may not have made it through the storm life sent your way. Times when someone close to you helped keep you on course when you began drifting away. Maybe it was with some words of encouragement... *"Hang in there!" "Don't quit!"* Perhaps an act of kindness... *"I paid the bill for you." "I brought you dinner."* Maybe it was your knowing others were praying for you.

48

Fair weather friends

There are those who we might call *"fair weather friends."* Those who will be friends as long as everything in life is fine. They are friendly for a time, but when adversity comes... when the skies grow dark and cloudy... they are nowhere to be found. Again Solomon writes,

> *Wealth brings many friends,*
> *but a poor man's friend deserts him.*
> *A false witness will not go unpunished,*
> *And he who pours out lies will not go free.*
> *Many curry favor with a ruler,*
> *and everyone is the friend*
> *of a man who gives gifts.*
> *A poor man is shunned by all his relatives-*
> *how much more do his friends avoid him!*
> *Though he pursues them with pleading,*
> *they are nowhere to be found.*
> Proverbs 19:4-7 (NIV)

Have you ever known any friends like that? Friends who only want to get something? Those who are more interested in something you can give them rather than having any interest in you personally? If you have, then you can really appreciate those who are friends like Luke.

The honesty of friends

One of the very special things about good friends is they will not only stick with us through storms, but they will always be honest with us. In their honesty they may even save us from a storm. Again Solomon in his wisdom tells us,

Faithful are the wounds of a friend,
But the kisses of an enemy are deceitful.
Proverbs 27:6

While no one likes to be wounded, or necessarily likes wounding another with something they have to say, understand that a friend, for our benefit, will sometimes have to wound us. If not, their honesty is compromised, and they are really no friend at all.

Do you want to have and be able to maintain good and honest friends? Friends like Luke? Take a good look at another wise principle from Solomon.

A man who has friends
must himself be friendly,
But there is a friend
who sticks closer than a brother.
Proverbs 18:24

That's not hard to understand. If you want to keep your friends and perhaps have even more friends... be a good friend yourself. Stick close to those going through storms. Stay by their side. Encourage them just like Luke and his friendship with Paul.

Paul, this great apostle and hard worker for the cause of Christ, needed friends in his life. He needed others to keep him going through all the difficulties he experienced. We all do. We all need good friends.

One songwriter from years back wrote of a very special friend we all have. A friend who will stick closer to us than a brother. A friend who we can always turn to for help and encouragement. A friend who will always be honest with us in the words he has given to us. A friend who will not forsake us when life's storms come upon us. The friend is Jesus. A friend who gave His life for us.

What a friend we have in Jesus,

All our sins and griefs to bear;

What a privilege to carry,

Everything to God in prayer.

O what peace we often forfeit,

O what needless pain we bear,

All because we do not carry,

Everything to God in prayer.

Have we trials and temptations?

Is there trouble anywhere?

We should never be discouraged,

Take it to the Lord in prayer.

Can we find a friend so faithful,

Who will all our sorrows share?

Jesus knows our every weakness,

Take it to the Lord in prayer.[12]

When Storms Come

6

A Survival Tip

But He said to them,
"Why are you fearful,
O you of little faith?"
Then He arose and rebuked
the winds and the sea.
And there was a great calm.
Matthew 8:26

With his good friend Luke by his side, Paul and the rest of the crew and passengers were in the midst of a life-threatening storm. The men on board the ship were losing any hope of survival. And as the strong winds and high seas continued rocking the ship and everyone's nerves, Paul continued talking to the men on the ship. Earlier we read how he had told them they should have listened to him. Now, as he continues speaking to them, he begins to offer some words of encouragement. Exactly the type of words folks need to hear when they are going through life's storms. As the crew and passengers all feared the worst, Paul talked to them of their great chances for survival.

> *"And now I urge you to take heart, for there will be no loss of life among you, but only of the ship. "For there stood by me this night an angel of the God to whom I belong and whom I serve, "saying, 'Do not be afraid, Paul;"*
>
> Acts 27:22-24a

I get the feeling in reading these verses that even Paul, the great apostle, the great proclaimer of the gospel, the one who himself had been through many trials, persecutions, and difficult situations, might have had some doubts himself about survival due to this storm's fierce intensity. Notice what the angel told him. *"Do not be afraid, Paul."*

It is interesting to me that Paul could have easily traveled to Rome as a free man, as he did to any of the other cities he visited. If God had so chosen, the journey there could have been without incident. Yet, he would go to Rome as a prisoner. The journey to that city would be accompanied with disaster and danger. He would reach Rome by way of this dangerous and life-threatening storm.

God, as powerful as He is, with all of His providential control over the creation, could easily have taken away the storm... but He didn't. Think about that! Maybe as yet He has not taken away the storm you're going through. That doesn't automatically mean you won't survive it. It does not mean that it is certain you will not reach your ultimate destination.

The angel told this storm-tossed weary apostle, *"Do not be afraid."* It is almost as if he was saying... *"God is still with you Paul! He is still in control!"* And guess what faithful but weary Christian, He is still with you! Even though it seems dark, and even though the tempests of life are raging, God is still with you. God is still in control. As Paul would later write,

> *What then shall we say to these things? If God is for us, who is against us?*
> Romans 8:31 (NASB)

I think most of us would love to have an angel appear to us during a difficult time and say those words... *"Do not be afraid."*

- When we are waiting for test results from a doctor...
  "Do not be afraid."
- When we are left to grieve the loss of a loved one...
  "Do not be afraid."
- When the disease is not going away...
  "Do not be afraid"

> *'Do not be afraid, Paul; you must be brought before Caesar; and indeed God has granted you all those who sail with you.'*
> Acts 27:24b

What a comforting message sent by God to a weary and storm ravaged apostle, delivered by a celestial messenger. A message that provided Paul renewed faith and hope, as well as a special reminder of God's incredible love and presence.

It was the angel's message to Paul, which changed his message to the crew of this ship. Earlier he had given them a message of doom and destruction...

> *"Men I perceive that this voyage will end with disaster and much loss, not only of the cargo and ship, but also our lives."*
> Acts 27:10

Now, after receiving the message from God, delivered by the angel, Paul's message is one of hope!

> *"And now I urge you to take heart, for there will be no loss of life among you, but only of the ship."*
> Acts 27:22

In these two messages are seen two very common perspectives among people. The first is a horizontal perspective. It looks at the situations of life from a human perspective. It is based on what are seemingly known facts and circumstances. It is a perspective that while sometimes accurate, is often hopeless.

The other perspective is one that is vertical. It looks towards God. It is based neither on fact nor circumstance, but on God's word. It is a perspective that offers faith, hope, and love. The very things the crew of this ship needed. It is the perspective we all need when dealing with life's storms.

This vertical perspective of hope was made possible for us by the cross of Jesus. His death, burial, and resurrection has accomplished for those who are in Christ, a living hope. The cross forever stands, like a lighthouse in the storm, signaling direction in life. If you are lost in the sea of life... look to the cross. It is there you will find faith, hope, and love. And with faith, hope, and love, comes a whole new perspective.

A survival tip

I told you earlier about a survival tip for handling the storms of life; well, we have finally reached that part of the journey. In many respects, it all has to do with perspective. Look closely at Paul's next words. They contain great advice for dealing with life's inclement weather...

> *Therefore take heart, men, for **I believe God that it will be just as it was told me.*** [13]
> Acts 27:25

There it is! The survival tip? Believe God... no matter what else is happening... no matter how dark it may be... Believe God that in the end, it will turn out exactly as it was told you.

Paul knew in the end he would survive. He knew he would reach his destination. He knew he would arrive safely. Despite the current circumstances, desperate and dark as they were, he believed God. That's what we need to do. Believe God! When we believe God... when we are putting our trust in Him... no matter what the weather of life may be like, we are able to hold to those three important anchors: faith, hope and love. And remember,

- With faith comes vision and direction.
- With hope comes endurance.
- With love comes comfort.

Amidst the storms that come our way in this life, believe God that in the end it will be just exactly as it was told us. And think what He has told us! All the promises He has made to the believers, His children. The apostle Peter called them exceeding great and precious promises.[14]

Promises Promises Promises

Take some time to consider some of the wonderful promises that await the child of God. I have listed several here as a means of providing faith, hope, and love. These are promises we can count on, just as we are told. The Hebrew writer tells us that He who promised is faithful.[15] God will fulfill what He has promised.

A Promise of Life...

A promise of life in heaven... a life free of all the cares and concerns which so often trouble us here... a life free of storms!

> *This is the promise which He Himself made to us: eternal life.*
> 1 John 2:25 (NASB)

> *In the hope of eternal life, which God, who cannot lie, promised long ages ago.*
> Titus 1:2 (NASB)

A Promise of Hope...

Hope is crucial for survival. Without hope, people give up. God has given us an eternal hope. Something to look forward to with great anticipation. Peter called our hope, a living hope.

> *Blessed be the God and Father of our Lord Jesus Christ, who according to His abundant mercy has begotten us again to a living hope through the resurrection of Jesus Christ from the dead, to an inheritance incorruptible and undefiled and that does not fade away, reserved in heaven for you.*
> 1 Peter 1:3-4

A Promise of Confidence...

Not a confidence merely in ourselves, but we can have confidence in God. We can depend upon Him to deliver what He has promised. We can have confidence that He hears our prayers, and our cries for help when life's weather becomes cold and bitter.

> *Now this is the confidence that we have in Him, that*
> *if we ask anything according to His will, He hears us.*
> 1 John 5:14

A Promise of Forgiveness...

It is a wonderful feeling to be forgiven. To know a wrong you have committed against someone has been released and forgotten. Through the shed blood of Jesus Christ and our obedience to the gospel, we can be forgiven of our sin.

> *If we confess our sins, He is faithful and just to*
> *forgive us our sins and to cleanse us from all*
> *unrighteousness.*
> 1 John 1:9
> *"For I will forgive their iniquity, and their sin I will*
> *remember no more."*
> Jeremiah 31:34b

A Promise of Peace...

To have peace is a wonderful experience. It is to enjoy serenity, quiet, and calmness. The turbulent weather of life can be anything but peaceful. Life's storms will steal away the serenity and calmness of life. They bring things like chaos, turmoil, confusion, and anxiety. Yet, rather than being without peace and not knowing how to obtain it, Paul gives us a wonderful formula for enjoying not just any kind of peace, but the peace of God. A peace, which he says, surpasses all understanding. If we will follow Paul's formula, we can find and maintain peace, even in storms.

> *Be anxious for nothing, but in everything by prayer*
> *and supplication, with thanksgiving, let your requests*
> *be made known to God; and the peace of God, which*

61

surpasses all understanding, will guard your hearts and minds through Christ Jesus.
                    Philippians 4:6-7

A promise of love...

A love from God that is unconditional. A love so strong and committed that He sent His Son to this earth to die for us. A love greater than any love we could find on this planet among our friends and family.

Paul described God's love for us so well, in his Roman letter, writing essentially about life's storms. And he tells us they cannot take away God's love.

> *Who shall separate us from the love of Christ? Shall tribulation, or distress, or persecution, or famine, or nakedness, or peril, or sword? As it is written: "For Your sake we are killed all day long; We are accounted as sheep for the slaughter." Yet in all these things we are more than conquerors through Him who loved us. For I am persuaded that neither death nor life, nor angels nor principalities nor powers, nor things present nor things to come, nor height nor depth, nor any other created thing, shall be able to separate us from the love of God which is in Christ Jesus our Lord.*
>   Romans 8:35-39

On and on we could go, with promise after promise. And we can have confidence as God's children, that He will fulfill every promise He has made. You can count on that, understanding that we as His children must live up to the conditions of the promises. One of the conditions being that we practice this survival tip...

believe God. Therefore, believe Him that in the end it will be just as it was told you. I believe these promises are without a doubt...

- A source of calm in the storms of life.
- A light in times of darkness.
- A certainty when everything else seems so uncertain.
- A security when we're feeling insecure.

In fact, these promises, and the confidence that we can have in God fulfilling them, through our Savior Jesus Christ, are anchors in times of storms. An enduring hope, when everything else seems hopeless. The Hebrew writer said it all so well.

> *In the same way God, desiring even more to show to the heirs of the promise the unchangeableness of His purpose, interposed with an oath, so that by two unchangeable things, in which it is impossible for God to lie, we who have taken refuge would have strong encouragement to take hold of the hope set before us. This hope we have as an anchor of the soul, a hope both sure and steadfast and one which enters within the veil.*
> Hebrews 6:17-19 (NASB)

I realize this survival tip will not take away the pain you are feeling. It will not answer all of your questions. It does not take away the tears. But believing God and holding on to these promises will give us endurance. It will keep our faith and hope alive. It will remind us of His great love for us. Faith, hope, and love. There they are again. Those three important anchors for this often rough voyage through life. To quote from Paul...

> *"Therefore, take heart men, for I believe God, that
> it will be just as it was told me "* (And as it was
> told you)

This life will always be filled with difficult days, you know
that. But let us keep our spiritual eyes focused on God, and on
the promises. We must (despite life's often stormy weather),
keep focused on the promised life to come in heaven. That is our
final destination. That is where this "ship" you are sailing as a
Christian, though often storm-tossed, is heading!

Not an easy journey

At this point I can really appreciate Paul's next words to the
men on board the ship. He has just told them how he believed
God. He told them they would all survive. And just about the
time some of them might have started to smile and perhaps regain
some hope, Paul says,

> *"However, we must run aground on a certain island.*
> Acts 27:26

You can just picture these rain-soaked and weary sailors
looking at Paul like he was out of his mind! *"We're going to
crash!"* Some of them must have thought he was crazy. Others,
no doubt, were still discouraged.

That can be a real problem today. Many expect their voyage
through this life to be an easy one; and when it is not, they
become discouraged.

> *"I'm a Christian; why is this happening to me?"*
> *"They are good people; why is this happening to them?"*

64

In a sense, on our journey to heaven, we have crash-landed at times. We have run aground on occasion. The journey to reach heaven is not always easy. The skies are not always clear. The storms do come. That is why it is so important for us to remember to believe God, no matter what else may be happening in our lives. Believe Him, that in the end it will be just as it was told you.

When Storms Come

7

No Escape

*And as the sailors were seeking
to escape from the ship,*
Acts 27:30a

The storm we have been reading about during Paul's voyage to Italy just would not quit. On and on it kept going... day after day... night after night... a continual downpour of hard rain and strong winds. The crew and passengers on board the ship must have wondered if it would ever end.

Some of you know times like that in your life. Times when the winds and rain from life's storms have you drenched, soaked, and discouraged. Times when there doesn't appear to be any sign of the storm letting up. Times when life seems like a continual and constant downpour of difficulties and hardships. At times like that, we would all like a quick way of escape from the deluge. We would all like a way to overcome the storm's destruction. However, when storms come, there is often no easy way of escape. They must be courageously endured and patiently outlasted.

Losing courage and patience, some of the sailors on board the ship sought a way they could possibly escape the storm. So they contrived a plan. A quick way of escape from what they felt was certain doom. Apparently, in the sailor's minds, the constant rocking of the large ship and the continuance of the storm gave them little hope of survival. They had to devise a way of escape.

> *But when the fourteenth night had come, as we were driven up and down in the Adriatic Sea, about midnight the sailors sensed that they were drawing near some land.*
>
> Acts 27:27

Did you catch that? Fourteen nights! Imagine fourteen nights at sea in a storm of this magnitude. No wonder these men wanted off this ship! The bad weather was not going to quit, but they were.

> *And they took soundings and found it to be twenty fathoms; and when they had gone a little farther, they took soundings again and found it to be fifteen fathoms. Then, fearing lest we should run aground on the rocks, they dropped four anchors from the stern, and prayed for day to come. And as the sailors were seeking to escape from the ship, when they had let down the skiff into the sea, under pretense of putting out anchors from the prow,*
>
> Acts 27:28-30

What a plan! *"Let's pretend we're lowering the anchors. Then we'll jump into the skiff and get out of here!"* They wanted off the main ship and out of the storm. Thinking only of themselves, they were willing to leave behind the others on board the ship to face the storm's destructive force without their help.

There are those today who will often do the same kind of thing when life's difficult times come. They think only of themselves, and leave others to deal with the storm on their own. Their selfish thinking often finds them abandoning family and friends, at times even God. Either in actions or words, they say things like,

"You're on your own..."
"Let me out of here..."
"You can handle it..."
"I can't take it anymore..."

The sailor's planned escape from the ship would fail. Learning of their calculated escape, Paul warned Julius what would happen if they were to leave the ship.

Paul said to the centurion and the soldiers, "Unless these men stay in the ship, you cannot be saved." Then the soldiers cut away the ropes of the skiff and let it fall off.

Acts 27:31-32

You can just imagine the look of lost hope on the faces of the sailors as they watched the skiff drop into the rough seas and out of their sight. They had worked so hard to secure it and get it on board. Now they watched as it was quickly swallowed up and destroyed by the sea. They saw what they thought was their only means of hope and survival disappearing into the deep waters of the sea. Watching the skiff sink must have left them fearful, frustrated, hopeless, disappointed, discouraged. You know the feelings. They are common during the difficult weather of life.

- When your options seem to be disappearing.
- When your plans are not working.
- When an empty sinking feeling begins overtaking you.

Despite what Paul had told them earlier about how he believed God that they would all be safe; they still did not believe. And if you put yourself in their position... why should they believe Paul? Believe this Jewish prisoner? What kind of credibility could he possibly have? They would much rather trust in themselves, and their chances for survival (against the immense storm) in the small boat. Their foolish thinking saying, *"We can handle it!"*

Many people today have a hard time believing another one-time Jewish prisoner. One who holds the answers for surviving and dealing with life's storms, Jesus Christ. He offers a way of escape from certain destruction. Yet, some wonder what credibility could He possibly have? One who was taken prisoner... Abandoned by His closest friends... Crucified on a cross... They would much rather trust in themselves.

These sailors who were seeking an easy way out, and many people today, would do well to heed the words of Solomon.

> *Trust in the Lord with all your heart,*
> *And do not lean on your own understanding.*
> *In all your ways acknowledge Him,*
> *And He will make your paths straight.*
> Proverbs 3:5-6 (NASB)

In essence, Solomon is speaking of our survival tip. Believe God. Trust in Him. He will help you through life, and through the many storms that accompany it.

Words of encouragement

After fourteen nights of being tossed about, with men ready to jump ship, what everyone really needed to hear was some encouraging words. And, that is what Paul is going to speak to them.

Encouraging words can be so helpful at difficult times. The hard part is knowing the right words to say. To find just the right words which will comfort and encourage. Positive words which will provide strength, but not sound meaningless or too cliché.

Paul knew what to say. He knew they were hungry and discouraged. So he encourages them to eat and reminds them of how he believed God. We might say, he gave them a survival tip.

> *And as day was about to dawn, Paul implored them all to take food, saying, "Today is the fourteenth day you have waited and continued without food, and eaten nothing. "Therefore I urge you to take nourishment, for this is for your survival, since not a hair will fall from the head of any of you." And when he had said these things, he took bread and gave thanks to God in the presence of them all; and when he had broken it he began to eat. Then they were all encouraged, and also took food themselves. And in all we were two hundred and seventy-six persons on the ship.*
>
> Acts 27:33-37

There they were, all two hundred and seventy-six people aboard this ship, bouncing and rocking on the rough seas. The wind and the rain was beating hard upon them. And in the middle of it all Paul offers some words of encouragement. It was exactly what they needed to hear at just the right time. They were hungry, tired, and ready to jump ship.

Paul tells them to take time out and eat! He reminds them again of how he believed God. *"Not a hair from the head of any of you shall perish."* I love the way Luke records the effects of Paul's urging them to eat... *"All of them were encouraged..."*

If there is anything people going through storms need to hear, it is words of encouragement. They need the reassurance found in words of hope and comfort. Sometimes it may be as simple as encouraging them to eat. At other times it may take words of encouragement to undergird their faith and give them strength and endurance. To remind them of the importance of faith, hope, and love.

Solomon knew the importance of encouraging words and their power to inspire and motivate when people are discouraged and storm-tossed. He gave several proverbs showing us the power of encouraging speech.

A soothing tongue is a tree of life,
But perversion in it crushes the spirit.
Proverbs 15:4 (NASB)

A man has joy in an apt answer,
And how delightful is a timely word!
Proverbs 15:23 (NASB)

Pleasant words are a honeycomb,
Sweet to the soul and healing to the bones.
Proverbs 16:24 (NASB)

Like apples of gold in settings of silver
Is a word spoken in right circumstances.
Proverbs 25:11 (NASB)

Land ahead

Finally after days and days on the rough sea, land was in sight! Can you believe it? Hold on tight, here is how Luke records their landing...

*So when they had eaten enough, they lightened the ship
and threw out the wheat into the sea. Now when it was
day, they did not recognize the land; but they observed
a bay with a beach, onto which they planned to run the
ship if possible. And they let go the anchors and left
them in the sea, meanwhile loosing the rudder ropes;
and they hoisted the mainsail to the wind and made for
shore. But striking a place where two seas met, they ran
the ship aground; and the prow stuck fast and remained
immovable, but the stern was being broken up by the
violence of the waves. Now the soldiers' plan was to kill
the prisoners, lest any of them should swim away and
escape. But the centurion, wanting to save Paul, kept
them from their purpose, and commanded that those
who could swim should jump overboard first and get to
land, and the rest, some on boards and some on broken
pieces of the ship. And so it was that they all escaped
safely to land.*

Acts 27:38-44

What a scene! Stuck in the bay, the ship is being broken into
pieces by the huge waves. Though it certainly made no sense to
the crew and passengers, the ship's destruction would lead to
their landing safely on shore. It was God making provision for
the people. His divine providential hand was right there, an
unexpected blessing in the midst of their terror.

They may not have been aware of God's presence, but He was
right there with them. As they floated to the safety of land on the
broken pieces of wood from the ship, God's presence was all
around them. The whole scene was a remarkable picture of His
divine grace.

When life doesn't seem to make sense, when the vessel of your
life appears to be stuck, and doomed for destruction, look for

God's provision. It may not be obvious... it may not be what you expected... but His way is always the way that ultimately leads to rest and safety.

The prophet Jeremiah knew this. As he stood amidst the rubble and ash of what was once Jerusalem, destroyed because of continued disobedience and rebellion, that weeping prophet described the greatness of God's faithfulness, even at that desperate time. Jeremiah wrote:

> *This I recall to my mind, Therefore I have hope.*
> *Through the Lord's mercies we are not consumed,*
> *Because His compassions fail not.*
> *They are new every morning;*
> *Great is Your faithfulness.*
> *"The Lord is my portion," says my soul,*
> *"Therefore I hope in Him!"*
> *The Lord is good to those who wait for Him,*
> *To the soul who seeks Him.*
> *It is good that one should hope and wait quietly*
> *For the salvation of the Lord.*
> Lamentations 3:21-26

Notice that Jeremiah says, *"The Lord is good to those who wait for Him."* Often our trouble is... we do not like to wait for Him! We want the torrent to be over, now! We want answers! *"It is good that one should hope and wait quietly."* When our *"ship"* is being torn apart it is hard to be quiet, it is hard to keep hope alive.

Here is where our survival tip becomes so important. Believe God! Know that His faithfulness is great. Even in the midst of destruction and ruin, unexpected blessings may often be found.

The crew and passengers of this torn apart ship, though unaware, experienced first hand, God's remarkable grace. One by

76

one they would each make it to the shore, all two hundred and seventy-six of them. Some swimming, some hanging on for dear life to pieces of what used to be the ship. Washing up on the beach, soaking wet and covered with sand, perhaps they turned and fearfully watched the final destruction of the ship as it remained stuck in the bay, a sight that must have brought about feelings of utter hopelessness. *"Now what do we do?"*

However, their fear and feelings of hopelessness would soon give way to the obvious conclusion. They were all safe! The ship did not make it… but they did. Paul was right. He had told them what God had said. And everything happened just as it was told him. God always keeps His promises. Great is His faithfulness! What was it that Paul said earlier?

"I believe God, that it will be just as it was told me."

8

On Our Way Home

To an inheritance incorruptible
and undefiled
And that does not fade away,
Reserved in heaven for you.
1 Peter 1:4

We made it! Despite the rough weather we have been reading about, we finally made it. A comforting thought, isn't it? Knowing you have made it somewhere? Though the way was difficult and the weather treacherous, reaching a planned destination is a rewarding experience. There is a feeling of accomplishment in arrival.

- For the college graduate, it's finishing the course and receiving the degree... *"I did it!"*
- For the athlete, it's finishing the race... *"I made it!"*
- For many, it's simply surviving a storm... *"It's over!"*

That reminds me of some words written by Paul in what may have very well been his last letter. Written from a Roman dungeon, awaiting his execution, Paul knew he had almost reached his destination. He knew he was on his way home.

> *I have fought the good fight, I have finished the race, I have kept the faith. Finally, there is laid up for me the crown of righteousness, which the Lord, the righteous Judge, will give to me on that Day, and not to me only but also to all who have loved His appearing.*
>
> 2 Timothy 4:7-8

Paul knew exactly where he was going. You can hear his confidence in those words. He knew he was heading home. Despite the difficult circumstance he found himself in at the time, he knew that ultimately he would arrive safely. You can almost hear him shouting in those verses... *"I did it!" "I made it!" "It's over!"*

For you and I to experience that same kind of joy and excitement in the accomplishment of arriving, we must have a planned destination. A direction to head and a planned course for how we are going to get there. Unfortunately, many in life do not seem to have a direction. They are not sure where they're going. And that can lead to some pretty stormy weather in life!

Where are you heading?

What is your planned destination as you journey through this life? Where are you heading? If you do not have a direction, you need one. You need somewhere to point your *"ship."* You need some place to navigate towards, a goal to look through the clouds in search of, a destination place far beyond the storms to look forward to. Direction and goals in life are so important.

And, while having a destination in mind is important, perhaps far more important is making sure it is the right destination. Make sure your ultimate destination in life offers the joy and rewards you are expecting upon arrival. Some destinations may appear like great places to direct ourselves towards, but ultimately they can often lead only to destructive weather.

Many have made their direction in life one of obtaining wealth. In so doing they have found that the expense of achieving that wealth was not necessarily worth the price paid to achieve it. The pursuit of wealth has often caused some to sacrifice families, friends, personal integrity, and at times, even God. In the end finding the happiness it promised was not forever. It is a pursuit that can many times create some stormy weather in life.

In much the same way, some have set their sights on destinations such as... fame, power, education, and a multitude of other directions and goals that have only provided them with temporary satisfaction. There is certainly nothing wrong in pursuing any of those things, depending of course on how we choose to pursue them. However, understand that the things of this life, while often enjoyable, will never provide you with a lasting fulfillment and happiness.

For the Christian, the destination is heaven. It is where we have set our sights. With God's word as a chart and compass we have set sail toward an eternal home. And even though this life may often be filled with difficulties, cloudy days and stormy skies; the Christian can look forward with confidence to something much better. An eternal home with better weather. A promised home where there is no storms. We can rejoice in the fact that we are on our way home.

Blessed be the God and Father of our Lord Jesus Christ, who according to His abundant mercy has begotten us again to a living hope through the resurrection of Jesus Christ from the dead, to an inheritance incorruptible and undefiled and that does not fade away, reserved in heaven for you, who are kept by the power of God through faith for salvation ready to be revealed in the last time. In this you greatly rejoice, though now for a little

> *while, if need be, you have been grieved by various trials,*
>
> 1 Peter 1:3-6

Peter tells us in those verses that even though we are grieved by various trials (call them the storms of life), even though we experience hardships and difficulties in this life... we can still rejoice in the fact that a promised home in heaven awaits those in Christ. And what a home it will be! A home where there will be...

- No more sickness
- No more pain
- No more hospitals
- No more funerals
- No more death
- No more storms

Almost makes you want to go home right now doesn't it? Just thinking about the joy and happiness that awaits us in heaven. And you know what? It is all waiting for us! God has promised it! And I believe God, that it will be just as it was told me... and you.

However, until we get home... we have to keep surviving the constant downpours of this life. Our journey here will often be difficult. There will be times when things will not seem to make sense. There will be times of pain and suffering. And, there will be times of loneliness and despair. Along the journey of our life will be times of discouragement and loss. These times (and others like them) are the storms of life. They have come in the past, they are here now, and they will be here in the future. But keep in mind, our journey through this life is only temporary. This is not our final stop, it is only an often rough ride through heavy seas to our eternal home above.

When the weather gets too rough, remember to undergird. If the temperature gets too cold, find a place to winter. If the rumbling echoes of the thunder get too loud, don't lose faith. If the lightening strikes too close, hang on to your hope. Through it all, remember God's love. Keep your eyes on that promised home. Keep sailing... Keep your direction... And hold on tight... There is rough weather ahead... But we are on our way home.

> *O they tell me of a home far beyond the skies,*
> *O they tell me of a home far away.*
> *O they tell me of a home where no storm clouds rise,*
> *O they tell me of an unclouded day.*

When Storms Come

9

Jesus And Storms

And the men marveled, saying,
"Who can this be, that even the winds
and the sea obey Him?"
Matthew 8:27

We have just worked our way through a very powerful storm. The record of which is found within the pages of the Bible. Interestingly, it is not the only storm found in the pages of Scripture. The Bible has its share of accounts of stormy weather. Real and powerful storms which ushered certain individuals through high winds and serious downpours.

Who could ever forget the great deluge that Noah and his family went through? How about the turbulent downpour that led to Jonah being thrown overboard into a furious sea? There was the time Elijah (through prayer) called down a heavy rain on the earth as a sign that he was a prophet of God.

Of the various storms recorded in the Bible, two of them involved Jesus and His disciples. In the high winds and pounding rain of these torrents which He and his disciples faced are some valuable and always timely lessons for us to learn. Lessons that can help us in dealing and coping with life's storms today.

Jesus, Himself was no stranger to life's inclement weather. He saw them come upon others and He experienced the same. One by one people would come to Him seeking relief from life's difficult weather. Multitudes full of hurting and desperate people would flock to Him in search of miracles.

- The demon possessed.
- The sick and diseased.
- The lepers.
- Those who could not walk.
- Those who had lost loved ones to death.

Matthew tells us that Jesus, seeing a multitude of people who had come to Him, was moved with compassion, and healed their sick.[16] On another occasion, Jesus, arriving at the place where they had buried Lazarus (the brother of Mary and Martha), seeing the grief and pain they felt at the loss of someone close to them, Himself began to weep, because of His love for Lazarus.

The night in which He would be arrested, Jesus experienced a storm of His own. Entering into the garden of Gethsemane, knowing what was about to happen to Him on the cross; Jesus fell to the ground on His face, sorrowful and deeply distressed, praying to the Father, *"Let this cup pass from Me."* Three times He prayed, and three times the answer came back, *"No."*

Jesus found strength in prayer and His determined obedience to the Father, expressed in these words, *"Not My will but Yours be done."* He walked out of that garden strong and committed, ready to give His life on the cross. A sacrifice that would rescue all who will avail themselves of it.

Because of what Jesus saw and what He Himself experienced, Jesus knows what it is like when life's storms come upon us. The Hebrew writer described His wonderful ability to understand what you and I go through in this life in the familiar words,

> *For we do not have a high priest who cannot sympathize with our weaknesses, but One who has been tempted in all things as we are, yet without sin.*
> Hebrews 4:15 (NASB)

Because of our great high priest, Jesus Christ, and because He understands, look at the writer's conclusion and exhortation to us...

> *Therefore let us draw near with confidence to the throne*
> *of grace, so that we may receive mercy and find grace*
> *to help in time of need.*
> Hebrews 4:16 (NASB)

That verse contains great instruction for those times when life's storms beat hard upon us. When the boisterous sounds of thunder can be heard, and lightning flashes across the sky, when life finds us fearful, discouraged, and full of doubts, draw near with confidence to Jesus. It is there we will find the shelter of mercy and grace to help us in that time of need. He is the calming force of life's high winds and seas.

Why are you fearful?

Fear is a common feeling during life's storms. The uncertainty and doubt they often bring can be very frightening. They are like the loud sounds of thunder echoing in the skies which can bring shivers to even the strongest. It was the feelings of fear that found the disciples drawing near to Jesus on several occasions.

Once, finding themselves caught at sea in a storm, they turned to Jesus. It had been a long day of teaching. Multitudes of people had gathered around Jesus. Some to hear Him teach, some perhaps for a miracle of some kind. It was a scene common in His earthly ministry. And when Jesus and His disciples were finished taking care of the needs of the people, they launched out to sea in a boat, and Jesus no doubt tired from the days events, fell asleep.

Now when He got into a boat, His disciples followed Him. And suddenly a great tempest arose on the sea, so that the boat was covered with the waves. But He was asleep. Then His disciples came to Him and awoke Him, saying, "Lord, save us! We are perishing!"

Matthew 8:23-25

Notice that the text says this tempest came upon them suddenly, without warning. That can be very frightening. Just as in life, the sudden occurrence of storms leaves little time to prepare for the downpour. One moment the skies are clear, the next dark and threatening. That is where these disciples found themselves. They were obviously frightened by the storm's fierceness. This is somewhat surprising when one realizes that some of these men were fishermen. They were certainly no strangers to the sea. This sudden cloudburst, however, is like nothing they had ever seen. The boat was being covered with waves. They were being tossed about from the large swells, hanging on for dear life.

And where is Jesus while all of this is going on? He is asleep! In Mark's gospel he records the disciples asking Jesus, *"Teacher, do you not care that we are perishing?"*[17]

Some today may feel like God is asleep during the storms they have to endure in life. That He doesn't care. That He isn't concerned. Life's storms have caused many to question...

- *"Where are You God?"*
- *"Do You hear me?"*
- *"Why won't You answer me?"*
- *"Don't you care what is happening to me?"*
- *"Please hear me God!"*

Despite what anyone may think, God is not asleep! Like Jesus in the boat with these disciples, God is right there with you. It is usually us who abandon or go to sleep on Him!

Storms are a part of this life. But you say, *"I'm a Christian!"* That's great! But that does not make you immune to life's inclement weather. Think about it... here were the disciples of Jesus, just like you and me today at times, caught in the middle of a life-threatening situation. *"Lord, save us! We are perishing!"*

> *But He said to them, "Why are you fearful, O you of little faith?"*
> Matthew 8:26a

The men on the boat had all but lost three essential ingredients for getting through life's storms... faith, hope, and love. They were dominated by fear. Fear had stolen away their faith. With faith gone, so was hope. Love may have also been in doubt as they fearfully wondered how Jesus could sleep at such a desperate time. After all, *"How could He do that?"*

Jesus calmly asks them, *"Why are you fearful, O you of little faith?"* They had forgotten who was with them. Jesus was right there in the boat! Yet, rather than seeking His help, in essence, they rebuked Him! Their words to Jesus could be translated, *"Wake up Lord!"* It is the same thing many do today when life's storms arrive; they blame God. They rebuke Him. Jesus, however, rebukes the storm.

> *Then He arose and rebuked the wind, and said to the sea, "Peace, be still!" And the wind ceased and there was a great calm. And they feared exceedingly, and said to one another, "Who can this be, that even the wind and the sea obey Him!"*
> Mark 4:39-41

With a few words, Jesus brings about a calm, to the storm and no doubt to the disciples. *"Peace be still!"* How wonderful it would be to just be able to speak those words when the storms of life come our way, and to have them quickly disappear. It would be nice... but we can't.

And yet, while you and I can not make life's storm go away with a few simple words, we can seek the One who calmed a storm with His words. He is our great high priest. Seek Him! Turn to Him! Run to Him just as the disciples ran to Him. It doesn't mean the skies will immediately clear up, but knowing who is *"on the boat"* with us can give us a wonderful feeling of peace. *"Peace be still."*

David wrote of the peace that can come through the power of the Lord's voice in his beautiful words from Psalm twenty-nine.

*The voice of the Lord is over the waters; the God of glory
thunders, the Lord thunders over the mighty waters.
The voice of the Lord is powerful; the voice of the Lord is
majestic.
The voice of the Lord breaks the cedars; the Lord breaks in
pieces the cedars of Lebanon. He makes Lebanon skip like
a calf, Sirion like a young wild ox.
The voice of the Lord strikes with flashes of lightning.
The voice of the Lord shakes the desert; the Lord shakes
the desert of Kadesh.
The voice of the Lord twists the oaks and strips the forests
bare. And in His temple all cry, "Glory!"
The Lord sits enthroned over the flood; the Lord is
enthroned as King forever.
The Lord gives strength to His people; the Lord blesses His
people with peace.*

Psalm 29:3-11 (NIV)

Why did you doubt?

The storm we have just looked at was not the only one which Jesus and his disciples found themselves having to deal with. There was another storm recorded in scripture; with still more application for you and me. Once again the day had been a busy one. There was yet another multitude of people with needs to be met. They were sick and hungry. And after a lesson on how to feed a multitude of people with five loaves and two fish, the disciples learn another lesson about dealing with storms.

> *Immediately Jesus made His disciples get into the boat and go before Him to the other side, while He sent the multitudes away. And when He had sent the multitudes away, He went up on a mountain by Himself to pray. Now when evening came, He was alone there. But the boat was now in the middle of the sea, tossed by the waves, for the wind was contrary.*
>
> Matthew 14:22-24

Notice that Jesus sent those disciples out into the boat, and essentially out into a troubled sea. As we have previously noted, being followers of Jesus does not make us immune from life's storms. We must learn, as these disciples needed to learn, to faithfully endure them.

While Jesus went to pray, Matthew tells us the boat with the disciples was in the middle of the sea being tossed about by the waves. As the boat rocked and creaked, they must have wondered where Jesus was. It was getting late. Perhaps they questioned, *"How long is this going to last?"*

You have probably felt the same way at times. Full of doubts, worries, questions... *"When is this going to end? When is God going to answer my prayer?"* It could be He has answered your prayer. We sometimes forget *"No"* is an answer. It is not the answer we usually want, but it is an answer. It was the answer Jesus received in Gethsemane. God in His infinite wisdom answers prayers in our best interests. We may not understand... we may not like the answer... but understand the prayer is still answered; God is still with you.

Along these lines, I want you to notice a small, but important, detail that Mark gives us in his gospel account of this storm.

> *And seeing them straining at the oars, for the wind was against them, at about the fourth watch of the night, He came to them, walking on the sea; and He intended to pass by them.*
> Mark 6:48 (NASB)

Jesus saw them straining at the oars. He knew what was going on. The word *"straining"* in that verse comes from a Greek word which spoke of torture during a judicial trial. Another idea of the word was any kind of severe distress, or to be harassed.[18] It sounds exactly like life's storms and what they often put us through. They become torturous and strenuous trials, which find us weary and worn, looking for relief. Life's storms can bring some to a point of questioning, *"Where is God?"* They bring us severe distress. At times, it seems like life is harassing us. Yet, notice again, Jesus saw them straining. He knew what they were going through, and He knows what we are going through.

Like us, the disciples must have wondered if Jesus knew. Finally... during the fourth watch of the night... somewhere between three and six in the morning... Jesus appeared. What a welcome sight!

Now in the fourth watch of the night Jesus went to them, walking on the sea. And when the disciples saw Him walking on the sea, they were troubled, saying, "It is a ghost!" And they cried out for fear. But immediately Jesus spoke to them, saying, "Be of good cheer! It is I; do not be afraid."
Matthew 14:25-27

What comforting words. *"Be of good cheer! It is I; do not be afraid."* These are words we need to remember during our times of fear in the midst of the bad weather of life. Our high priest is there for us. He is listening. He understands. He is watching. You are not alone!

One disciple on board this boat was seemingly overjoyed at the sight of Jesus. That was Peter. Perhaps he just wanted off the creaking and wave-tossed ship. Maybe he wanted to show Jesus how great his faith was. Whichever, he cries out to Jesus,

And Peter answered Him and said, "Lord, if it is You, command me to come to You on the water." So He said, "Come." And when Peter had come down out of the boat, he walked on the water to go to Jesus. But when he saw that the wind was boisterous, he was afraid; and beginning to sink he cried out, saying, "Lord, save me!" And immediately Jesus stretched out His hand and caught him, and said to him, "O you of little faith, why did you doubt?" And when they got into the boat, the wind ceased.
Matthew 14:28-32

Peter started off great. But, once he saw how strong the tempest really was he became afraid and doubted. At that point he began to sink. Jesus asked him, *"Why did you doubt?"* When life's storms come our way, we too may start off great. Yet, after re-evaluating its fierceness, we also may begin to doubt.

When that feeling of fear begins to come upon you. When you like Peter, feel yourself beginning to sink in doubt. Keep your eyes on Jesus. Though the winds may howl and the thunder loudly and confidently rumbles, keep your faith, hope, and love alive. Remember the survival tip... Believe God, that it will be just as it was told you.

Where are you building?

A chapter on Jesus and storms would not be complete without noticing, however briefly, His advice on preparing for storms. We need to understand that it is a fact of life that difficult periods will likely come our way. Life's storms hit everyone. Part of being able to properly endure them, involves some advanced planning.

Jesus, in His sermon on the mount, gave us a parable that has become a popular song for young children in Sunday school. Yet the lessons contained within this parable are such, that perhaps adults should be singing that little children's song. *"The wise man built his house upon the rock..."* Notice what Jesus tells us about preparing for life's storms.

> *"Therefore whoever hears these sayings of Mine, and does them, I will liken him to a wise man who built his house on the rock: "and the rain descended, the floods came, and the winds blew and beat on that house; and it did not fall, for it was founded on the rock. "But everyone who hears these sayings of Mine, and does not do them, will be like a foolish man who built his house on the sand: "and the rain*

descended, the floods came, and the winds blew and beat on that house; and it fell. And great was its fall."

Matthew 7:24-27

Being able to successfully endure the rains, floods, and winds of life has a great deal to do with what type of foundation we are building upon. On what are we resting our hopes and dreams? On the instability and weakness of the sand? The sand being the temporal things of this life. If so, then when life's winds and rains beat hard upon us, they will easily wash our hopes and dreams away. There is no strength and dependability on a sandy foundation.

We must build upon a sure and stable foundation. We must build upon a faith, hope, and love in Jesus Christ. The One who calmed storms with His voice. The One who could walk on water. The One who died upon a cross. The One who Himself faithfully endured life's storms. The writer of the book of Hebrews said it well,

Therefore, since we have so great a cloud of witnesses surrounding us, let us also lay aside every encumbrance, and the sin which so easily entangles us, and let us run with endurance the race that is set before us, fixing our eyes on Jesus, the author and perfecter of faith, who for the joy set before Him endured the cross, despising the shame, and has sat down at the right hand of the throne of God. For consider Him who has endured such hostility by sinners against Himself, so that you may not grow weary and lose heart.

Hebrews 12:1-3 (NASB)

Look to Jesus. Consider what He endured. Consider what others have endured, and why their faith either failed or triumphed when the storms of life came upon them. With faith, hope, and love as anchors, practice the survival tip... do your best to keep the vessel of your life on course.

10

After The Storm

My beloved spoke, and said to me:
"Rise up, my love,
my fair one, and come away.
For lo, the winter is past,
The rain is over and gone.
Song of Solomon 2:10-11

W hat comforting words to think about... *"After the storm."* What encouraging words to be able to boldly speak, *"The storm is over!"* Looking out on the vast horizon of life you can finally see the backside of the clouds. They are finally moving away from you. And breaking its way through the parting of the clouds is the warmth and light of the sun. A more than welcomed feeling and sight. The clear skies and sunshine are good indicators, that the storm is over... it is really over!

After the storm, there comes a time to assess any damage left behind from the winds and rain. It is time to make the necessary repairs and move on. Time to prepare for the next gathering of clouds and rain. Most importantly, it is a time to enjoy the sunshine! A time to rejoice and enjoy the good weather of life.

It is sometimes hard to believe when we are in the midst of one of life's downpours that there could ever be an end to all the trouble, but endings do come. Often it just takes time. The dark skies and clouds usually do not hang around forever, eventually they move on, though not always soon enough.

I like how the poetic words of Solomon describe the refreshing and wonderful times of life, after the storm.

My beloved spoke, and said to me:
"Rise up, my love, my fair one, And come away.
For lo, the winter is past,
The rain is over and gone.
The flowers appear on the earth;
The time of singing has come,
And the voice of the turtledove
Is heard in our land.
The fig tree puts forth her green figs,
And the vines with the tender grapes
Give a good smell.
Rise up, my love, my fair one, And come away!
(Song of Solomon 2:10-13)

Isn't that beautiful? There is some great advice in those verses for enjoying life again, after the storm.

- Rise up... *Get going!*
- It is time to sing... *Pick a favorite tune!*
- Smell the beauty of nature... *The flowers are waiting!*
- Come away... *It is long deserved!*

Storms tend to keep us locked up and sheltered, but now that it is gone, escape! *"Rise up my love... come away..."*

Noah was one who knew all about being locked up during a downpour. He knew about that special time, after the storm. For forty days and forty nights while the Earth's first deluge poured forth an abundance of rain, Noah and his family were tossed about in that first ship. Even when the rains finally stopped, Noah had to wait for the waters to recede so that dry land would be accessible.

It would be close to a year's time before Noah and his family would leave the ark. But at long last, the ending came. The dove which Noah had previously sent out twice, only to have it return both times finding no dry ground, at last never came back, signaling the joy of dry land.

After the storm, God spoke to Noah informing him of a promise that is still evident today.

> *And God said: "This is the sign of the covenant which I make between Me and you, and every living creature that is with you, for perpetual generations: "I set My rainbow in the cloud, and it shall be for the sign of the covenant between Me and the earth.*
> Genesis 9:12-13

When nature's storms have finished delivering their sometimes fierce and frightening punch, a rainbow can often be seen in the clouds. Usually signaling it is over. A beautiful reminder for us of God's divine presence and His faithfulness to His wonderful promises.

I do not know where life finds you right now. It could be that your reading of these words finds you in the midst of a terrible torrent in life. You are longing for the time when it will be, *"after the storm."* When, like Noah, you can send out that dove and have it never come back. That time when once again, you can enjoy the good weather of life. I wish I could tell you that time will be soon, it might be... but no one knows for sure.

Until the downpour is over, the skies clear, and the rainbow is seen, remember the importance of faith, hope, and love. As we have mentioned, they are essentials for surviving life's many storms. Keep them securely in your grips, because the rough weather of life can easily steal them away from you. In the difficulties and seeming endlessness of life's inclement times, faith can begin to doubt... hope can often dwindle... and love can be challenged. Throughout the journey of this life, no matter what, do not forget the survival tip... believe in God

Conclusion

Throughout this book we have watched as Paul and the men on board the ship with him were tossed about in a life-threatening storm. Though fearful and about out of hope, when it was all finally said and done, they survived. The landing was rough, but they made it through the perilous journey. Perhaps it was with this voyage in mind that Paul later penned the words,

> *And not only that, but we also glory in tribulations,*
> *knowing that tribulation produces perseverance; and*
> *perseverance, character; and character, hope.*
> Romans 5:3-4

After the storm, Paul knew surviving and properly handling it gave him a stronger faith. It produced in him more hope. It kept him focused on God's unending love. The same can be true for us as we, too, strive to hold on to faith, hope, and love in the midst of the downpours life sends our way. Paul himself said it well as he closed his beautiful chapter on love.

> *And now abide **faith**, **hope**, **love**, these three; but*
> *the greatest of these is love.*
> 1 Corinthians 13:13

May these three essential anchors... faith, hope, and love, abide with you always as you journey through this life. In times of clear and sunny skies... and in the frightening and difficult times when you are surrounded with dark and ominous clouds... When Storms Come.

The Lord bless you and keep you;
The Lord make His face shine upon you
And be gracious to you;
The Lord turn His face toward you
And give you peace.
Numbers 6:24-26 (NIV)

When Storms Come

Notes

1 J.K. Alwood, *O They Tell Me of a Home.*

2 Emphasis mine.

3 Acts 19:21.

4 2 Timothy 4:21a (NASB)

5 2 Timothy 4:13.

6 Isaac Watts, *O God, Our Help in Ages Past.*

7 Ephesians 4:16

8 Acts 27:1a, emphasis mine.

9 Acts 27:2, emphasis mine

10 Acts 27:3a, emphasis mine

11 See 2 Corinthians 11:23-28.

12 Joseph Scriven, *What a Friend We Have in Jesus.*

13 Emphasis mine.

14 2 Peter 1:4.

15 Hebrews 10:23

16 Matthew 14: 14.

17 Mark 4:38b (NASB)

18 Walter Bauer, F. Wilbur Gingrich, and Fredrick W Danker, *A Greek-English Lexicon of the New Testament and other Early Christian Literature* (Chicago: University of Chicago Press, 1957), 134.

Order Form

To order additional copies of this book please complete the following information.

Send to: (Please print)

Name _____

Address _____

City, State, Zip _____

____ Copies of 'When Storms Come' @ $7.95ea. _____

Shipping and handling @ $2.00 per book _____

California residences add 7.75% tax _____

Total amount _____

Make checks payable to: LLMK Publishing
                        1905 N. Sundown Lane
                        Anaheim, Ca. 92807

(Please send no cash)